KIDS IN THE KITCHEN

TESCO

Recipes developed by: Valerie Barrett, Cathy Dunn, Jenni Fleetwood
Additional assistance from the Tesco Consumer Kitchens
Written by Jenni Fleetwood
Illustrated by Anni Axworthy

Published exclusively for Tesco Stores Ltd,
Delamare Road, Cheshunt, Herts, EN8 9SL
by Cathay Books, 59 Grosvenor Street, London W.1

First published 1986

© Cathay Books 1986

ISBN 0 86178 394 8

Printed in Hong Kong

We would like to thank the following who were
concerned in the preparation of the book

Series Art Director Pedro Prá-Lopez
Photographer Chris Crofton
Stylist Hilary Guy
Food prepared for photography by Jennie Schapter
Special editorial help Cathy Dunn
Other help Nick and Tom
Editors Camilla Simmons and Isobel Greenham

Contents

Introduction   page 5
Safety and good sense   page 6

Cooking Terms   page 8

Lunch Boxes   page 12

Supper Dishes   page 18

Picnics   page 28

Puddings   page 34

Party Food   page 42

Edible Gifts   page 54

Index   page 64

NOTE

Standard spoon measurements are used in all the recipes

1 tablespoon = one 15 ml spoon
1 teaspoon = one 5 ml spoon
All spoon measures are level

All eggs used in the recipes are sized 3 or 4 (standard) unless otherwise stated.

In each recipe the quantities are given in both
metric and imperial measurements. Be sure to follow either set,
not a mixture of both.

Following the success of the first 12 books we produced in the Tesco Cookery Collection, we are delighted to be adding 8 new titles to this exciting series. As before, it is the close contact we have with our customers and the feedback we have had through our Consumer Advisory Kitchens which has helped us to select these latest titles. Each one focuses on an area in which our customers have shown particular interest and contains practical background information on the chosen subject together with a wide selection of carefully tested recipes, each one illustrated in colour.

Readers who enjoyed *Cooking for Kids* will be thrilled with *Kids in the Kitchen* — a book written this time for the kids themselves. With their catchy names, step-by-step illustrations, cartoons, and delicious ingredients the recipes will have an instant appeal to children of all ages. Try them on Jungleburgers for a suppertime special, Popeye power packs for a healthy lunch, a Loch Ness monster for pudding or a Punk lady for a partytime mocktail. There's also a section on cooking terms — explaining methods through easy-to-follow illustrations, and a high level of safety and kitchen sense is maintained throughout.
I hope parents will be delighted by the results of their kids' efforts in the kitchen. Enjoy your cooking, kids!

Carey Dennis, chief home economist, Tesco Stores Ltd.

Introduction

Kids in the kitchen is a collection of recipes chosen by children who love to cook. All the recipes are easy to understand, with simple step-by-step instructions, so that even the child who has never cooked before will soon be turning out super snacks, suppers and treats. The book is intended for 8 to 12 year olds but many of the simpler recipes are equally suitable for younger children, provided they are adequately supervised. Teenagers and grown-ups will enjoy the book too. Clear sketches and photographs help to make the explanations easy to follow and there are lots of useful tips on the simplest and safest ways of preparing food. Many of the cookery terms grown-ups take for granted are hard for children to understand, so these words are marked with shading on them in the recipes and there's a special section on these terms on page 8.

Safety is the most important consideration when kids are in the kitchen and it is vital that children read the section on Safety and good sense on pages 6 and 7 before they start to cook. We recommend they have a grown-up standing by when they first start to cook. To help the kids remember the **kitchen code**, potentially dangerous situations are underlined in the methods. Red exclamation marks in the illustrations also warn of times when special care should be taken or a grown-up asked to help.

There is a wide range of recipes and a swift glance at the method to check underlined areas will help a parent decide which recipe to choose to suit the child's degree of ability.

Mocktails are easy to make and great fun to drink – they are made without the use of heat, so this would probably be a good starting point for beginners.

Safety is essential but it is not the only aim of the book. Instilling good kitchen sense is also an important aspect and young cooks are encouraged to work methodically and tidily and to leave the kitchen as their parents would like to find it.

The principles of healthy eating have not been neglected either. The lunch box section, for instance, includes a seafood salad, filled pitta breads, mini quiches and a warming chicken soup. Pasta, jacket potatoes, fresh vegetables and fruit, yoghurt and cheese have all been included and the aim has been to provide dishes which are fun to cook and form part of a well-balanced diet.

Children who tried out some of the recipes made many useful suggestions – lunch box food had to be reasonably durable to withstand satchel bashing; party food must include savoury as well as sweet items.

Let the kids into your kitchen – you won't regret it!

SAFETY AND GOOD SENSE

A kitchen is not a kindergarten — you've got to be careful when handling hot foods, sharp knives and electrical equipment. Please read this section carefully before you start to cook and return to it from time to time. To help you remember the **kitchen code**, you'll find safety reminders throughout.

Safety Reminders

If part of a recipe is underlined, that means you should be extra careful and ask your Mum or Dad to help you until both you and they feel confident you can cope. Red exclamation marks on the illustrations mean the same thing — take great care. Look at the recipe for Buttons and bows on page 18. You'll see the word 'carefully' is underlined in Step 3, when you pour the hot sauce over the pasta bows. The red exclamation mark by the drawing and the underlining of the word are to remind you to take care to avoid spilling the hot mixture and scalding yourself.

Shaded words for cooking terms

Some of the words in the recipes, such as 'grated' in the list of ingredients to Buttons and bows and 'drain' in the method are shaded — this shows that if you don't know what the words mean you can look them up in Cooking terms on pages 8-11.

The kitchen code

- Always ask permission before you start to cook.
- Wash your hands thoroughly.
- Put on an apron or an old shirt of your father's with the sleeves cut to size (fathers get attached to old clothes so be sure to ask first).
- If you have long hair, tie it back. Only a caterpillar is worse than a hair in your food.
- Choose a recipe you know you can handle and read it through before you begin. Look up any words you don't know. Ask a grown-up to help you with any underlined areas and to check your oven or grill settings.
- Set out all your ingredients and utensils before you start.
- When you use a knife, always work on a chopping board or you may cut the worktop. Be careful how you hold the knife. Always lift a knife by its handle and cut away from yourself so that if the knife slips it will not matter (see picture and caption). When washing or drying a knife,

When cutting, always work on a wooden board. Hold the knife firmly with the blade away from you and keep your other hand well clear of the cutting edge. This photograph shows you how to cut celery for boats — fill them with mayonnaise, add cocktail flags and you can sail them on the Seaside salad (see page 12).

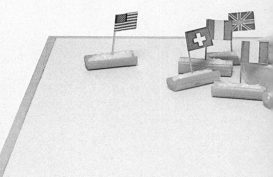

always wipe it from the back.
- When cleaning vegetables it is better to scrub rather than peel them as the goodness is near the surface. Keep a separate brush for this.
- When you pick up anything hot, a saucepan, baking dish or grill pan, for instance, or something which contains hot liquid, such as a kettle, always wear oven mitts.
- Saucepan handles should never be allowed to stick out on the hotplate — you may overturn a pan and scald yourself. Also, if you are cooking something in a pan with a lid, make certain any holes in the lid are turned away from you so you are not scalded by escaping steam.
- If you need to use electrical equipment such as an electric whisk or a food processor, always ask permission and have a grown-up help you. *Never* touch any electrical equipment or a plug with wet hands.
- If you spill anything on the floor clean it up straight away or you may slip and fall. This is dangerous any time but if you are carrying something hot or breakable you could have a nasty accident.
- Don't forget to turn hotplates, oven or grill off when you have finished.
- Clean up as you go along if possible and always leave the kitchen clean and tidy.

Cooking terms

MEASURING

For all the recipes, quantities are given in metric measures, with imperial measures in brackets. Oven temperatures are given in degrees Celsius, degrees Fahrenheit and Gas Marks. You should stick to either metric or imperial measures. Where tablespoons are used, you should use a level 15 ml measuring spoon. A **measuring jug** is usually marked in millilitres on one side and fluid ounces on the other. Put the jug on a flat surface so that your eye is level with the jug and slowly pour in the liquid to be measured until it reaches the required mark.

We usually use **scales** to measure dry ingredients. Beginners will find it easiest to use scales like those sketched below, showing both metric and imperial measures. Before you begin, make sure the pointer is on zero, then add the dry ingredient to the pan until the pointer shows the exact amount you require. Do not look down on the dial – read it at eye level.

Cutting butter portions.
To cut a 250 g (8 oz) block of butter or margarine into eight portions of approximately 25 g (1 oz) in size, cut it in half and then in quarters as shown by the dotted lines in the sketch and then divide it in eighths, as shown by the solid cutting line.

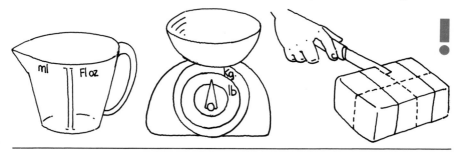

▲
TO BEAT means to mix with a strong, circular movement, with a fork, wooden spoon or balloon whisk.

◀ TO CORE means to remove the middle part of a fruit or vegetable. Use a knife if you are cutting the fruit or a special corer if removing only the centre.

TO DICE means to cut vegetables into square shapes, to make cooking quicker. To dice a potato, first peel it, then using a kitchen knife, *carefully* cut the potato in half. Put the potato half cut side down. Slice the potato lengthways, then turn it round and slice it across.

TO DRAIN means to pour off liquid from food. Pour into a colander or a sieve (use a sieve for chopped food). To keep the liquid, put the colander or sieve over a bowl.

TO DRIZZLE means to trickle a liquid such as melted butter or honey over the surface of food.

TO FLAKE means to break into pieces using a fork. The technique is usually used for fish.

TO FOLD means to add one mixture to another and then very gently turn them over and over using a metal spoon rather than a wooden one. This type of movement helps to trap air into the mixture, keeping it very light and fluffy. You usually do this with mixtures involving egg whites.

◀ TO GRATE means to cut food into small bits by rubbing it on a grater. Hold the grater firmly in one hand and the food in the other. Always watch your fingers!

Note: Turn over the page and you will find more explanations for cooking terms.

TO GREASE means to coat an ovenproof dish or baking tray with a little fat to prevent the mixture sticking during cooking.

TO BREAK an egg, tap it gently against the rim of a bowl until the shell cracks in the middle. Using your fingers, pull the 2 halves apart (don't squash them!) and let the egg drop into the bowl.

TO KNEAD means to squash and squeeze a mixture such as fondant paste so that it becomes soft. Use the heel of your hand or clench your fist and use your knuckles to push the mixture back and forth.

TO ROLL dough or pastry, place it on a wooden board or clean work surface lightly sprinkled with flour. Use a rolling pin to roll out the dough evenly to a thin flat sheet.

▲
TO RUB fat into flour is a useful thing to learn because you do it when making pastry. You need cool, *clean* hands for the job. When the ingredients are in the bowl, put your hands together with a little of the fat and flour mixture between the fingertips. Rub the mixture between your fingertips until it looks like fine breadcrumbs. Repeat until all the fat has broken down.

▲
TO SEPARATE an egg means to remove the yolk from the white. An easy and fun way to do this is to break the egg into a saucer, put an egg cup over the yolk and then, taking care not to let your hands slip, pour the egg white into a clean, dry bowl.

▲
TO SHRED means to cut into ribbon-like strips. To do this to lettuce or a cabbage portion, slice down just as if you were cutting bread very thinly.

▲
TO SIFT means to pass a dry ingredient through a sieve (wet ingredients such as sauces are STRAINED through a sieve). Put the sieve over a bowl, add the dry ingredient and gently shake until it has all gone into the bowl.

TO SIMMER means to cook steadily over medium heat. The liquid should not boil but bubbles should form gently on the surface of the liquid.

TO WHISK means to beat a mixture in order to trap bubbles of air. This is done with a rotary whisk, an electric whisk or a balloon whisk. ▼

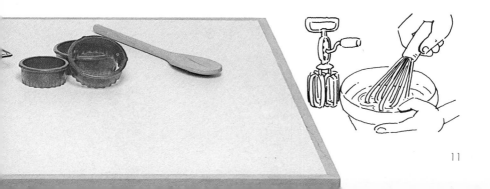

11

Seaside salad

For 2 you need

100 g (4 oz) pasta shells
1 teaspoon vegetable oil
½ × 198 g (7 oz) can tuna fish in brine
2 celery sticks, scrubbed and sliced
1 × 5 cm (2 inch) piece cucumber,
    washed and diced
1 red apple, diced

FOR THE DRESSING
2 tablespoons mayonnaise
2 tablespoons natural yoghurt
2 teaspoons lemon juice
salt and pepper

saucepan ● colander ● large bowl ●
spoon ● jam jar

1 Cook the pasta shells in the saucepan, following the instructions on the packet. When cooked, drain off all the water by carefully pouring the shells into the colander. (Do this over the sink!) Shake the colander gently and then put the shells back in the pan. Add the oil and stir. This keeps the shells separate. Set aside to cool.

2 Drain the fish, throwing away the liquid from the can, and put it in a large bowl. Flake it roughly. Add the cooked pasta shells and the sliced celery and diced cucumber and apple.

3 Make the dressing by putting all the ingredients in a small clean jam jar. Stir the mixture, close the lid, and shake. Now pour the dressing on to the tuna mixture and stir it well.

4 Spoon the salad into 2 plastic bowls with well-fitting lids. Store overnight in the refrigerator. Just before you leave for school slip one bowl in your lunch box with some wheat crackers and a fork or spoon and add an apple or pear for afters. If there's only one of you you can save the other helping for tomorrow or give it to a friend.

It says close the lid tightly.

12

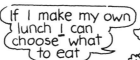
If I make my own lunch I can choose what to eat

with CHEESY BITES

Chunky chicken soup

For 2 you need

2 slices wholemeal or granary
  bread
25 g (1 oz) Edam cheese, grated
1 × 425 g (15 oz) can cream of
  chicken soup
1 × 198 g (7 oz) can sweetcorn
4 mushrooms, wiped clean and finely
  sliced
50 g (2 oz) frozen peas
2 tablespoons milk

saucepan ● wooden spoon ● 2 small
vacuum flasks ● small knife ● foil

1 Turn grill on to heat up. Toast bread slices on one side only under grill. Remove from grill and sprinkle untoasted sides with grated cheese. Pop back under grill till cheese is melted and bubbly. Put on a plate to cool. Turn the grill off.

Left: Chunky chicken soup with cheesy bites; Right: Seaside salad

2 Open cans and tip them both into the saucepan. Add the mushrooms, peas and milk. Put over medium heat, use the wooden spoon to stir now and then till hot – about 7-10 minutes. Carefully divide the soup between the 2 vacuum flasks – or if there's only one of you, keep half the mixture in the refrigerator for tomorrow.

3 Chop the toasts into small squares and wrap them in foil. When you pour your soup into your cup, sprinkle the cheesy bites on top and eat with a spoon.

Quiche-me-quicks

 akes 8 mini-quiches

100 g (4 oz) plain flour
salt and pepper
50 g (2 oz) butter or margarine, cut
    into cubes
2 tablespoons cold water

FOR THE FILLING
½ tablespoon vegetable oil
2 streaky bacon rashers, rinds and
    fat cut off, cut into squares (use
    scissors)
1 egg
3 tablespoons milk
25 g (1 oz) Cheddar cheese, grated

1 medium-sized and 1 small bowl ●
small kitchen knife ● round-bladed
knife ● rolling pin ● pastry cutters ●
fork ● frying pan ● patty tin

1 Sift the flour, salt and pepper
into the medium-sized bowl.
Add the butter or margarine and
rub the fat into the flour.

2 Sprinkle the water on to the
mixture. Stir with the round-
bladed knife. Mix the dough with
your hands until it forms a ball.

3 Roll the dough out thinly on a
flat surface and cut into 8
circles with a 7.5 cm (3 inch) pastry
cutter. Put each round in one of the
hollows of the patty tin. Prick the
bottom of each pastry circle with a
fork. Turn on the oven to 200°C or
400°F or Gas Mark 6.

4 Make the filling. Put the oil in
the frying pan over low heat.
Add the bacon and fry very gently
for about 5 minutes till well cooked.

I've packed 3 quiches.
And I've packed 3 too.

and let the quiches cool in the tin for a minute or two before removing them from the tin (the round-bladed knife is best for this). When the quiches are cold, pack 2 or 3 of them carefully into your lunch box. If you pack a crumpled paper napkin around each quiche they won't bump into each other and break.

5 Break the egg into the small bowl. Add the milk and beat together using the fork. Add the cheese, cooked bacon and a little pepper. Divide the mixture between the 8 pastry cases.

6 Put the patty tin on the middle shelf in the oven and cook for 18-20 minutes until the filling in each quiche is cooked and golden brown. Carefully remove the tin (use oven mitts), turn the oven off

For a change put a piece of cream cheese flavoured with garlic (if you like it) or herbs on top of each quiche before putting it in the oven.

Or finely slice 4 mushrooms and add them to the egg mixture before pouring it into the pastry cases.

Quiche-me-quicks packed in a lunch box with fruit and yoghurt, ready for school

That only leaves 2 for me!

Packed pittas

For 2 people you need 2 pittas cut in half. They make ideal edible containers for packed lunches as they're easy to carry. Wrap them in a clean napkin and pop in your lunchbox.

Here are 2 tasty fillings. Warm the pockets on each side under a <u>medium grill</u> before you fill them (it's easier that way) or pack a filling inside 4 fresh bread rolls or muffins.

ausage surprise

1 small or ½ large sweet red pepper
2 cold grilled pork sausages
1 × 198 g (7 oz) can sweetcorn, drained
1½ tablespoons mayonnaise

small kitchen knife • teaspoon •
bowl • wooden spoon

1 Wash and dry the sweet red pepper and place it on a board. Cut it in half with the knife (if using a whole pepper) and scoop out and throw away the seeds, using the teaspoon. Cut the pepper into thin strips or squares and put them in the bowl.

2 Put the sausages on the board and slice them thinly. Add them to the bowl.

3 Add the sweetcorn to the bowl with the mayonnaise and mix well with the wooden spoon. Get the pitta bread pockets ready to fill with the mixture.

4 Spoon some of the mixture into each pitta pocket and pack 1 or 2 of the prepared pockets into your lunch box.

PS Pitta bread is best eaten fresh so make these on the day you plan to eat them.

opeye power packs

4 lean unsmoked bacon rashers, rinds and fat cut off
pinch of cayenne pepper
100 g (4 oz) frozen chopped spinach
225 g (8 oz) low-fat cream cheese
pepper
1 tomato, cut into cubes

kitchen tongs or fork • absorbent kitchen paper • saucepan • large sieve • wooden spoon • bowl • kitchen scissors

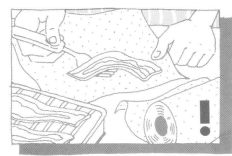

2 Cook the spinach according to the instructions on the packet. Put it in the sieve and drain very well, using the wooden spoon to press the spinach against the sides of the sieve to press out as much liquid as possible.

3 When the spinach is cold put it in the bowl. Then with the kitchen scissors carefully cut the bacon into small pieces and add to the spinach with the cream cheese and a little pepper. Beat with the wooden spoon until well mixed. Add the tomato and stir again.

1 Turn on the grill to heat up. Put the bacon on a grill rack and sprinkle with a little cayenne pepper. (Watch out – this stuff's dynamite!) Grill the bacon for about 4 minutes or until crispy. Using the kitchen tongs or fork transfer the bacon rashers to a sheet of absorbent kitchen paper to cool. Turn the grill off.

4 Spoon some of the mixture into each pitta pocket.

PS Putting the bacon on absorbent kitchen paper to cool is a good idea as the paper mops up the fat.

Below: Popeye power packs;
Underneath: Sausage surprise

Buttons and bows

For 4 you need

100 g (4 oz) pasta bows
25 g (1 oz) flour
25 g (1 oz) vegetable margarine
pinch of dried mustard
salt and pepper
450 ml (¾ pint) semi-skimmed milk
50 g (2 oz) frozen peas or button
    mushrooms
50 g (2 oz) canned sweetcorn
1 tomato, diced
1 × 99 g (3½ oz) can tuna, flaked
100 g (4 oz) Gouda cheese, grated
25 g (1 oz) fresh brown breadcrumbs

1 large and 1 medium-sized
saucepan ● colander ● balloon
whisk ● wooden spoon ● shallow,
heatproof 1.2 litre (2 pint) dish

1 Cook the pasta in the large saucepan according to the instructions on the packet. When it is cooked, drain it in the colander. Place the colander under the hot tap in the sink and run hot water through it. Shake it gently to drain again. Return the pasta to the pan.

2 Put the flour, margarine, mustard, salt and pepper and milk in the medium-sized saucepan. Put the pan over medium heat and use the balloon whisk to beat the mixture until the sauce boils and thickens. Turn the heat down to low, add the peas or mushrooms, sweetcorn, diced tomato, flaked tuna and half the cheese. Stir. Cook for 3 minutes.

3 Turn the grill on to heat up. Carefully pour the sauce mixture over the cooked pasta bows in the saucepan. Put it back on low heat for 2-3 minutes, stirring all the time with the wooden spoon until the mixture is hot.

4 Carefully pour the mixture into the heatproof dish. Mix the brown breadcrumbs with the rest of the grated cheese and sprinkle over the mixture. Pop under the hot grill for 3-4 minutes to brown but watch the topping carefully so that it does not burn. Turn grill off and serve straight away.

PS For 25 g (1 oz) breadcrumbs, you'll need 2 small slices of brown bread. You can use the food processor to make the crumbs, but ask Mum or Dad for help.

Cyclops specials

Enough for 2

2 slices wholemeal bread
2 teaspoons vegetable margarine
2 eggs
75 g (3 oz) Cheddar or Edam cheese,
   finely grated

butter knife ● 2 cups ● bowl ● metal
spoon ● rotary or electric whisk

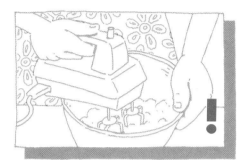

1 Turn grill on to heat up. Toast the bread on one side only under grill. Remove, spread untoasted sides with margarine. Put aside. Turn grill to medium.

2 Carefully separate the eggs. Put each yolk in a separate cup and whites together in the bowl.

3 Whisk the egg whites until stiff. Add the cheese and fold it into the egg whites with the metal spoon. Spoon the mixture on to the slices of prepared toast and shape into a nest. Slip an egg yolk carefully into the centre of each nest and place on the grill pan.

4 Gently slide the grill pan back under the heat and cook the toasts for about 2-3 minutes until set and golden brown. Turn grill off. Serve straight away.

Left: Buttons and bows; Below: Cyclops specials all ready to eat quickly

Jungleburgers

It's always fun making food look like something else and this recipe allows you to go wild making a jungle.

For 4 people you need

FOR THE JUNGLE
½ iceberg lettuce, shredded
4 slices of sweet red pepper, cut in half
25 g (1 oz) fresh bean sprouts
4 small celery sticks, with leaves

FOR THE BURGERS
450 g (1 lb) lean minced beef
¼ teaspoon dried basil
¼ teaspoon dried oregano
1 teaspoon fresh parsley or ½ teaspoon dried parsley
1 small onion, finely chopped
50 g (2 oz) fresh brown breadcrumbs (see **PS** on page 18)
salt and pepper
1 egg
2 teaspoons tomato relish

4 plates ● large spoon ● bowl ● cup ● kitchen tongs

1 First make your jungle floor. Get the serving plates and pile the shredded lettuce right to the edge of each plate, making sure you've left enough room to put the burgers on the same plate.

2 The slices of red pepper are slithery snakes so place them at various points on the jungle floor (not too near each other). The bean sprouts make brilliant logs so you

can scatter these all over the plate. Finally, of course, all jungles must have trees. So place 1 small celery stick on to each plate, they make perfect trees.

3 Turn the grill on to heat up. In a large bowl, mix together the beef, herbs, chopped onion and breadcrumbs. Add a little salt and pepper.

4 Beat the egg in a cup, add the tomato relish and pour into the beef mixture. Stir well.

5 Divide the mixture into 8 equal parts and shape them into burgers. Put the burgers on the rack of a grill pan and cook under a

medium heat for 20 minutes, turning them over once every 5 minutes, or until cooked the way you like them.

6 Turn the grill off and add 2 burgers to each plate. Add a small plastic wild animal or two if you like (wash them first). Serve straight away.

For a change: Serve with a mashed potato mountain. Make the mashed potato (asking Mum's advice). Pile some on to your plate, using a fork to mould quickly into a mountain – eat at once.

PS You can easily sprout your own beans at home. Buy special beans for sprouting at a health food store (garden seeds may have been treated with chemicals). **Alfalfa** beans work well or you could try **mung** or **soy** beans. You need a big glass jar with a wide neck, a piece of gauze or muslin and a rubber band. Spread 25 g (1 oz) of seeds out on a tray and check them over. Throw away any that are not perfect. Put the seeds in a strainer and rinse well under the cold tap. Then carefully slide them into the jar, trying not to damage them. Cover them with cold water, put the gauze on top of the jar and use the rubber band to hold it in place. Leave the beans overnight, then turn the jar upside down with the gauze still in place and pour off the water. Add more water to the jar but this time pour it away leaving the beans just damp. When you get home from school, rinse and drain the beans again. Do this once more before you go to bed. Between rinses, store the bean jar in a cupboard. The beans will soon start to sprout and after 4-7 days they will be ready to use. 25 g (1 oz) will serve 2 if they are to be the main part of a salad: or 4 if used with lots of other ingredients.

Jungleburgers with their impressive mashed potato mountains

Cowboy pies

Makes 12

1 × 450 g (1 lb) packet shortcrust
  pastry mix
1 tablespoon flour for sprinkling
100 g (4 oz) sausagemeat with herbs
1 × 220 g (7 oz) can baked beans in
  tomato sauce
2 tablespoons milk

---

bowl ● rolling pin ● 2 pastry cutters
● 12-hole bun tin ● spoon ● fork ●
pastry brush ● round-bladed knife

1 Turn on the oven to 200°C or
400°F or Gas Mark 6. Make
up pastry as packet instructions.

2 Sprinkle flour on your work
surface and rolling pin. Roll
out the dough until it is as thin as a
10p piece. Cut out 12 circles using a
pastry cutter a bit larger than the
hollows in your bun tin, and 12
slightly smaller circles, for lids. Put
the big circles into the greased tin.

Left: Hunky hot hats; Right: Cowboy pies

3 Put 1 teaspoon of
sausagemeat and 1
teaspoon of baked beans into each
pastry shell. Brush one side of each
lid with water and put them wet side
down on top of the filling. Pinch the
edges of both circles of pastry
together with your fingers to keep
the filling in.

4 Prick holes in each lid with a
fork and brush the top of
each pie with milk. Bake the pies in
the oven for 20 minutes until they
are golden brown. Remove them
from the oven (using oven mitts)
and turn the oven off. After letting
the pies cool for a minute or two,
remove them from the tin with the
round-bladed knife. Serve the
Cowboy pies hot or cold.

Hunky hot hats

akes 2-4

15 g (½ oz) vegetable margarine
1 onion, chopped into small pieces
4 large button mushrooms,
    wiped clean
4 medium-sized tomatoes,
    wiped clean
25 g (1 oz) Cheddar cheese, grated
25 g (1 oz) ham, cut into small pieces
pinch of dried basil
4 slices hot lightly buttered
    wholemeal toast cut into
    triangles, to serve

---

frying pan • wooden spoon • small
kitchen knife • teaspoon • bowl •
absorbent kitchen paper • shallow
ovenproof dish

2 Turn on the oven to 200°C or 400°F or Gas Mark 6. Put the tomatoes sideways on a board so the stalk end is to your left. Using the knife carefully slice off the right-hand end to make lids. Put the lids on one side. Scoop out the insides of the tomatoes, using a teaspoon. Chop the tomato insides – the pulp – and place in a bowl. Turn the tomato shells upside down and put them on absorbent kitchen paper to mop up any juice. Add the cooked onion and mushroom mixture to the bowl with the cheese, ham and basil. Stir until the ingredients are well mixed.

3 Arrange the tomato shells, cut sides up, in the ovenproof dish. Using the teaspoon, fill the shells with the cheese and ham mixture. Neatly put a mushroom cap on top of each tomato and cover with a tomato hat. Put the dish in the oven and bake for 10-15 minutes. Remove them from the oven (using oven mitts). Turn the oven off and serve the Hunky hot hats straight away on the small triangles of hot, buttered toast.

1 Put the margarine in the frying pan over medium heat until it has melted. Add the onion, and fry it until it is soft. Take the stalks off the mushrooms, but leave the caps whole. On a wooden board, carefully chop the stalks, stir them into the onions with the wooden spoon. Cook for 2 minutes, then turn off the heat.

Baked potatoes

Baked potatoes are always popular and they're very good for you, especially if you eat the skins. (Wash them well before you cook them.) Try them simply with butter, sour cream, low-fat soft cheese or yoghurt or sample one of the five fabulous fillings on this page and the next.

nough for 4

2 large baking potatoes, each about 225 g (8 oz)

---

vegetable brush ● absorbent kitchen paper towels ● kitchen knife ● baking tray ● spoon ● bowl ● fork

1 Turn on the oven to 200°C or 400°F or Gas Mark 6. Scrub the potatoes with the brush and then pat them dry with absorbent kitchen paper towels.

2 If you are planning to give the potatoes a fancy filling, place them flat on a board and with the knife carefully mark the skin around the middle of each potato as if you were going to cut them in half lengthways. If you are going to eat the potatoes whole, prick them all over with a fork.

3 Put the potatoes on the baking tray and cook them in the oven for 1-1½ hours.

4 Carefully remove the potatoes from the oven (use oven mitts). Keeping the mitts on, gently squeeze the potatoes to make sure they are soft. If not, pop

them back into the oven for 10-15 minutes more. **To serve the potatoes plain,** place them flat on a board and cut a big cross in the top of each potato. Squeeze the tops gently to open the crosses out. Add a little butter, low-fat soft cheese or natural yoghurt to the inside of the crosses. If you prefer to fill the potatoes, follow steps 5 and 6.

5 **For filled potatoes,** carefully cut them in half through the mark you made earlier. With the spoon carefully scoop out the potato flesh to leave a firm shell. Put the scooped-out potato in a bowl

and mash it with a potato masher or fork with the filling you've chosen. Pile the mixture back into the potato skins.

6 Heat through in the oven for about 10 minutes. Take out and add any topping suggested in the recipes that follow. Turn off the oven and serve the filled spuds straight away.

POTATO FILLINGS

Creamy mushroom mix

25 g (1 oz) butter
125 g (4 oz) button mushrooms, wiped clean and sliced
50 g (2 oz) low-fat soft cheese
pepper
4 teaspoons tomato relish (optional)

1 Melt the butter in a frying pan over medium heat. Add the mushrooms; fry for 3-4 minutes.

2 Scoop out the potato and mash it with the soft cheese (see basic recipe, step 5). Add the fried mushrooms and pepper.

3 Put back into the potato skins and heat through (see basic recipe, step 6).

4 Top each potato half with a teaspoon of tomato relish, if using, and serve.

From top: Tomato and cheese wonder; Bacon and chive chip; Apple and cucumber crisp; Creamy mushroom mix

Bacon and chive chip

6 bacon rashers, rinds and fat cut off
25 g (1 oz) butter
salt and pepper
2 tablespoons soured cream or
    natural yoghurt
2 teaspoons scissor-cut chives or
    spring onions

1 Grill and chop the bacon (steps 1 and 3 of Popeye power packs on page 17 tell you how to do this).

2 Scoop out the potato and mash it with the butter (see basic recipe, step 5). Add the bacon and a little salt and pepper.

3 Put back into potato skins and heat through (see basic recipe, step 6).

4 Top each potato half with some soured cream or yoghurt and a sprinkling of chives.

Apple and cucumber crisp

125 g (4 oz) cottage cheese
½ eating apple, cored and chopped
1 × 2.5 cm (1 inch) piece cucumber,
    washed and diced, but cut 3
    slices first
salt and pepper
watercress sprigs

1 Scoop out and mash the potato in a bowl using a potato masher or a fork (see basic recipe, step 5).

2 Mix it with all the filling ingredients.

3 Put it back into the potato skins and heat through (see basic recipe, step 6).

4 Serve with little sprigs of watercress and the cucumber slices.

Tomato and cheese melters

25 g (1 oz) butter
50 g (2 oz) Edam cheese, grated
1 slice of lean ham, chopped
2 tomatoes, diced, but cut some
    wedges first
pepper

1 Scoop out the potato and mash in a bowl with the butter (see basic recipe, step 5).

2 Gently fold in the cheese and add the ham and tomato and seasoning.

3 Put back into the potato skins and heat through (see basic recipe step 6).

4 Serve the hot potatoes with the tomato wedges that you have saved.

The best thing to put in a baked potato is your teeth.

26

Chicken in a ring

For 4-6 you need

1 × 250 g (9 oz) bag 'boil-in-the-bag' rice
4 tablespoons natural yoghurt
7 tablespoons mayonnaise
1¼ teaspoons mild curry powder
1¼ tablespoons mango chutney
1 teaspoon lemon juice
350 g (12 oz) cooked chicken, cut into bite-sized pieces
1 small sweet red pepper
50 g (2 oz) sultanas
25 g (1 oz) roasted peanuts, chopped

saucepan • colander • scissors • 2 large bowls • wooden spoon • small kitchen knife

1 Cook the rice in the saucepan following the instructions on the packet. When cooked, carefully remove the bag from the water and drain well. The safest way to do this is to pour the water with the bag into the colander in the sink. Let the bag cool a bit and then open it carefully with a pair of kitchen scissors and tip the rice into a large bowl. This is a tricky step and unless you are careful you could burn yourself so ask a grown-up to help. Set the bowl aside until the rice has cooled.

2 In the other large bowl, mix together the natural yoghurt, mayonnaise, curry powder, chutney and lemon juice with a wooden spoon. Stir in the chicken pieces until covered with sauce.

3 Cut the pepper in half carefully and with a teaspoon scoop out and throw away the seeds. Carefully chop the pepper and stir it into the rice. Add the sultanas and peanuts. Mix well.

4 Spoon the rice on to 4-6 plates, leaving a hole in the middle of each helping. Pile the chicken mix in the hole and serve.

Saddlebag specials

iker's bananas

4 large slices white bread
8 teaspoons peanut butter
4 small bananas

small kitchen knife • rolling pin •
butter knife

1 With the knife <u>carefully</u> cut the crusts off the bread.

2 Put a slice of bread on a board and roll the rolling pin over it to flatten it a bit. Do the same thing to the other slices.

3 Spread the bread with peanut butter. Peel the bananas, lay one on each slice of bread and then roll them up.

4 Wrap the banana rolls tightly in cling film and then in foil.

PS It is best to make these just before you leave for your bike ride as bananas can go brown.

gg and tuna triple-deckers

1 × 99 g (3½ oz) can tuna, drained
1 tablespoon thick natural yoghurt
1 tablespoon tomato ketchup
2 eggs, hard-boiled
1 tablespoon mayonnaise
8 slices brown bread,
    the same size as
4 slices white bread
50 g (2 oz) vegetable margarine

2 bowls • fork • butter knife

These sandwiches are perfect for picnics. Keep them in the refrigerator until just before you leave home or make them at the last minute. If you plan your cycle ride when the weather is hot, however, ask a grown-up about which fillings to choose as some foods shouldn't be left in a saddlebag for a long time on a hot day. Don't forget to pack some fruit in your bag, too.

1 Put the tuna, yoghurt and ketchup in a bowl and mash them together with the fork.

2 In the other bowl, mash the eggs. Add the mayonnaise and mix well.

3 Remove the crusts from all slices of bread. Spread half the slices of brown bread with margarine and all the slices of white bread. Put the prepared brown bread slices on one side. Then spread the remaining slices of brown bread with the egg filling and all the slices of white bread with the tuna mixture.

4 Put the sandwiches together. Start each one with a bottom deck of brown bread with egg, top with a slice of white bread and tuna and finish with a top deck of brown bread. Carefully cut the sandwiches into triangles. Wrap in foil. Put them in your saddlebag, ready for your journey.

B MX baps

Makes 4
50 g (2 oz) low-fat soft cheese
150 g (4 oz) Cheddar cheese, grated
1 small stick celery, finely chopped
1 × 2.5 cm (1 inch) piece cucumber, washed and finely chopped
4 wholemeal baps
1 carrot, peeled

bowl ● wooden spoon ● serrated knife ● grater

1 In a small bowl, beat the soft cheese and Cheddar together with the wooden spoon. Stir in the celery and cucumber.

2 Cut the baps in half and spread the cheese mixture over the bottom half of each one.

3 Grate the carrot coarsely. Put a little of the grated carrot on top of the filling on each bap. Cover with the tops. Wrap in foil.

Below: Egg and tuna triple-deckers; Biker's bananas; BMX baps; Fudge brownies, all set out for a picnic

Fudge Brownies

Makes 16

100 g (4 oz) butter
90 g (3½ oz) plain chocolate
100 g (4 oz) caster sugar
100 g (4 oz) self-raising flour
50 g (2 oz) walnuts or raisins,
    carefully chopped
2 eggs
2 tablespoons milk
50 g (2 oz) plain chocolate, coarsely
    grated, for topping (optional)

shallow cake tin, measuring 20.5 cm
× 20.5 cm (8 × 8 inches) •
greaseproof paper • saucepan •
wooden spoon • 1 large and 1 small
bowl • fork • round-bladed knife

1 First get your cake tin ready. Grease it with a small amount of margarine, cut a piece of greaseproof paper to fit into the bottom of it and then grease the paper. Put the butter and chocolate into the saucepan over *low* heat until melted. Stir all the time with the wooden spoon and take the pan off the heat as soon as the contents have melted.

You can see what Fudge brownies look like on page 29

2 Turn on the oven to 180°C or 350°F or Gas Mark 4. Put the sugar, flour and walnuts into the large bowl and mix well together with a wooden spoon. In another bowl beat the eggs and milk together with the fork. Add the egg mixture and the chocolate mixture to the dry ingredients (the sugar, flour and walnuts) and mix well with the wooden spoon.

3 Pour the mixture into the prepared tin and put in the oven for 35-40 minutes.

4 Using oven mitts carefully take the tin out of the oven and put it on a heatproof surface. Turn the oven off. Sprinkle the grated chocolate, if using, on the surface of the cake while it is still hot. Leave it for a few minutes to melt and then spread it with a round-bladed knife. Let it cool then cut into 16 squares to serve.

PS If you don't take these on a bike ride have them at teatime.

Why did the cowboy's car stop?

Wigwam wonders

Indian apples

For 4 you need
4 medium-sized cooking apples,
  wiped clean and cored
4 glacé cherries
25 g (1 oz) raisins, chopped
15 g (½ oz) dates, chopped
15 g (½ oz) walnuts, chopped
3 tablespoons thick honey
juice of 2 oranges

small kitchen knife ● ovenproof dish
● wooden spoon ● bowl ● teaspoon
● ladle or large spoon

1 Using the knife, carefully slit the skin around the centre of each apple.

Injun' trouble.

2 Turn the oven on to 180°C or 350°F or Gas Mark 4. Put the apples in the ovenproof dish and use the handle of the wooden spoon to push a glacé cherry to the bottom of the hole in each apple.

3 Mix the raisins, dates and walnuts together in the bowl and stir in 1 tablespoon of the honey. Use the teaspoon to fill the centres of the apples with this mixture. With the teaspoon, drizzle the rest of the honey over the apples. Now add the orange juice.

4 Bake in the oven for 40-60 minutes. 2 or 3 times during cooking remove the apples from the oven using oven mitts and spoon any juices in the pan over the the apples. The apples are done when they are puffy and soft inside. Remove from the oven using oven mitts and turn off the oven. Let the apples cool a little before you eat them or wrap them in foil if you want to keep them warm for a long time.

Over the page you will see a picture of Indian apples

Tom-tom drumsticks

Heap plenty for 4
8 ready-cooked chicken drumsticks

FOR THE SAUCE
1 × 213 g (8 oz) can chopped
    tomatoes
2 tablespoons brown sugar
2 tablespoons red wine vinegar
1 tablespoon Worcestershire or
    brown sauce
½ tablespoon soy sauce
½ teaspoon mild wholegrain
    mustard
½ green pepper
1 slice canned pineapple, chopped

saucepan ● wooden spoon ●
teaspoon ● small kitchen knife ●
shallow bowl ● kitchen tongs

1 First make the sauce. Put the tomatoes with the juice from the can into the saucepan. Stir in the sugar, vinegar, Worcestershire sauce, soy sauce and mustard with the wooden spoon.

2 Carefully cut the core from the green pepper, use the teaspoon to scoop out and throw away the seeds. Carefully chop the green pepper finely and add it to the saucepan with the chopped pineapple. Put the saucepan over medium heat until the sauce boils. Then turn the heat down a little and simmer the sauce for about 10 minutes until it is thick. Turn off the heat. Carefully pour the sauce into the shallow bowl and let it cool.

3 Carefully make 3 slits in each ready-cooked drumstick with the knife (this helps the sauce hold on to the chicken). Put the drumsticks on a plate or wicker basket lined with greaseproof paper (use kitchen tongs). Serve them with the dipping sauce.

For a change use the sauce as a warm dip for cooked frankfurters or even fish fingers.
PS Don't forget to give your guests paper napkins as holders for the drumsticks.

Totem rolls

For 4 you need

4 long seeded bread rolls
6 slices processed cheese
4 small slices lean ham
25 g (1 oz) soft butter
½ teaspoon dried marjoram

bread knife ● butter knife ● foil

1 Turn the oven on to 200°C or 400°F or Gas Mark 6. Carefully cut each roll into 2 slices lengthways, cutting almost but not quite through the roll.

From left: Indian apples ready to eat inside; Middle: Tom-tom drumsticks with the warm dipping sauce; Right: Totem rolls still in a foil boat

2 Put 2 slices of processed cheese to one side. Cut each of the remaining cheese slices into 4 strips and stick 2 cheese strips into each of the gaps in the rolls. Cut each slice of ham into 4 strips and tuck a ham strip behind each piece of cheese. Fold the ham strips in half if necessary.

3 Spread the butter over the top of each filled roll. Cut the remaining 2 cheese slices into thin strips and arrange them across each roll to resemble totem pole patterns. Sprinkle with a little marjoram.

4 Place each totem roll in a foil boat and put them in the oven for 10 minutes. Using oven mitts carefully take them out of the oven and wrap each totem roll in a second layer of foil to keep the heat in. Turn off the oven.

PS These are just as tasty if you eat them outside in the garden. They keep warm for quite a while, but still taste delicious when cold.
For a change use Edam cheese instead of the processed cheese and use thinly sliced tomato instead of the ham.

Sci-fi trifle

For a crowd (8-10) you need

1 × 410 g (14½ oz) can evaporated milk
1 × 125 g (4½ oz) packet sponge fingers
1 × 410 g (14½ oz) can loganberries or raspberries in natural juice or syrup
1 × 142 g (5 oz) packet raspberry flavoured jelly, in pieces
1 × 142 ml (5 fl oz) carton whipping cream
tube of Smarties

big glass serving bowl • *sieve* • *2 bowls* • *measuring jug* • *large spoon* • *saucepan* • *big mixing bowl* • *rotary or electric whisk*

1 Put the can of evaporated milk in the freezer to chill for 3 hours. Put 8 of the best unbroken sponge fingers aside and arrange the rest in the bottom of the serving bowl – a glass one looks terrific but ask if you can use it first.

2 Drain the loganberries or raspberries into the sieve, over a bowl. Put them on one side. Sprinkle about 4 tablespoons of the juice from the can over the sponge fingers in the bowl and pour the rest of the juice into the measuring jug. Add water until you have 300 ml (½ pint) of liquid. Pour this mixture into the saucepan, add the jelly and put over low heat, stirring with the spoon until all the jelly has melted. Carefully take the saucepan off the heat and leave until cool.

3 Put the evaporated milk in the big mixing bowl and whisk it until it thickens. You can use a hand whisk for this but it is easier to do with an electric whisk (used with permission, of course). Add the red jelly mixture a bit at a time, and carry on beating until frothy.

4 Arrange the loganberries or raspberries in the serving bowl on top of the sponge fingers. Spread them out so that they completely cover the biscuits. Very gently pour the frothy jelly mixture on top and carefully put the bowl in the refrigerator to chill for about 4 hours (while you wash up!).

5 Pour the cream into a bowl and whisk it until it thickens. With another spoon pile up the whipped cream in the centre of the jelly so that it resembles the dome of a flying saucer. But save a spoonful of cream for later.

6 Place the 8 best sponge fingers so that they rest on the edge of the cream dome and the edge of the dish. When you have done that add the blob of cream you've saved to the top of the cream dome. In the spaces between put coloured Smarties to look like portholes in the side of the space ship.

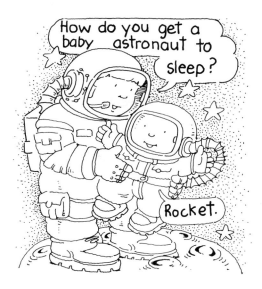

For a change try canned apricots with orange jelly or make up a combination of your own. Or you could use chocolate buttons instead of Smarties to decorate the flying saucer.

Sci-fi trifle decorated to look like an extra-terrestrial space ship ready to take-off

Igloo puddings

This serves 4

1 × 227 g (8 oz) can pineapple rings in natural juice, drained
12 small seedless grapes
2 egg whites
100 g (4 oz) caster sugar
1 small Arctic roll

baking tray ● foil ● bowl ● rotary or electric whisk ● large metal spoon

white mixture – the meringue – and use the spoon to make igloo shapes with snowy peaks.

1 Line the baking tray or grill pan with foil. Arrange 4 pineapple rings on the foil and fill the middle of each ring with 3 grapes. Turn on the grill to heat up.

2 In a large bowl, whisk the egg whites until stiff. Whisk in half the caster sugar, then fold in the rest of the sugar with the spoon.

3 Carefully cut the Arctic roll into 4 slices and put a slice on top of each filled pineapple ring. Use the back of the spoon to press them down firmly. Top each pudding with a quarter of the egg

4 Pop the baking tray or grill pan under the grill and leave for about a minute, until slightly golden on top. Watch the igloos all the time as they burn very easily. As soon as they are golden, carefully remove the baking tray or pan using oven mitts and turn off the grill. Using a fish slice, transfer each igloo to a small plate and serve straight away.

Fruity fools

or 4 you need

1 × 425 g (15 oz) can apricot halves in
   natural juice
1 × 150 g (5.29 oz) carton mandarin
   flavoured yoghurt
2 egg whites
1 tablespoon brown sugar
chocolate flakes and sugar stars,
   to decorate

sieve ● 2 large bowls ● wooden
spoon ● metal spoon ● rotary or
electric whisk ● 4 glasses

1 Drain the apricots by pouring
the contents of the can into a
sieve set over a bowl. Save the juice
(you could use it for a Mocktail –
read the **PS** at the end of this

recipe). Using the wooden spoon,
press the apricots through the sieve
into the bowl to make a purée. (You
can do the same thing very quickly
in a food processor but ask
permission before using one of
these and preferably ask a grown-
up to help you.)

2 Tip the mandarin yoghurt
into the purée and gently fold
it in using the metal spoon.

3 Put the egg whites in the
second large bowl and whisk
them until they are stiff. Add the
brown sugar and whisk again. Fold
this mixture into the apricot mixture.

4 Spoon into 4 glasses. Top
each glass with the
chocolate flakes and sugar stars.
Serve straight away.

PS You could make a Punk lady (see
page 52) using the apricot juice
instead of apple juice.

*Take a trip to the frozen north to eat,
right: Igloo puddings; or left: Fruity fools*

Loch Ness monster

For 4 you need

1 × 300 g (11 oz) can blackberries or
raspberries in natural juice or
syrup
1 teaspoon arrowroot or cornflour
3 large, firm curvy bananas
6 Matchmaker chocolate sticks
2 sultanas or raisins
4 scoops or chunks vanilla ice cream

sieve ● saucepan ● shallow
heatproof bowl ● balloon whisk ●
small kitchen knife ● skewer

1 Drain the juice from the fruit
you have chosen by pouring
into the sieve set over the
saucepan. Put the fruit into the
heatproof bowl and put to one side.

2 Using the balloon whisk, stir
the arrowroot into the juice.
Put the saucepan over medium
heat until the liquid boils, stirring all
the time until thick. Pour the sauce
over the berries and cool.

3 With the knife, <u>carefully</u> cut
the bananas to look like a

Loch Ness monster (the picture
shows you how). Break the
matchmaker chocolates into 1 cm
(½ inch pieces). With the skewer
<u>carefully</u> put a shallow hole into the
head and body of the monster then
push the Matchmaker chocolate
sticks into the holes to make spikes.
Push a sultana or raisin into each
side of the head to make eyes. Eat
any spare banana!

4 Pour the sauce on to a large
serving plate to look like
water at night time. Put the banana
monster into the middle arranging it
to look like the one in the picture.
Make rocks around the monster,
using scoops of ice cream. Eat the
pudding straight away before the
ice cream melts.

Must'nt get messy eating Nessy.

Marble fondue

Before you make the marble fondue arrange the fruit dippers on a big plate. Give everyone a good supply of cocktail sticks to use as spears for dunking the fruit dippers in the hot chocolate mixture.

Plenty for 4

175 g (6 oz) plain chocolate, broken into squares
75 g (6 oz) white chocolate, broken into squares
1 × 170 g (6 oz) can evaporated milk

FOR DIPPING
chunks of apple and pear, orange segments, pineapple cubes, glacé cherries, banana slices

2 heatproof bowls ● 2 saucepans ●
2 wooden spoons ● serving bowl ●
skewer ● cocktail sticks

1 Put the plain chocolate and white chocolate in separate bowls and set each bowl over a saucepan of hot water.

2 Pour half the evaporated milk into each bowl. Put the saucepans over medium heat so that the chocolate in each bowl melts very slowly. Stir each bowl occasionally with a wooden spoon.

3 When all the chocolate has melted, <u>carefully</u> pour half the white chocolate into a warmed serving bowl. Pour on all the plain chocolate and top with the rest of the white chocolate. Use the skewer or the handle of a teaspoon to draw through the mixture to make a marble pattern.

4 Serve the marble fondue straight away with the plate of fruit dippers.

Left: Loch Ness monster swimming among the rocks; Right: Marble fondue with dippers

39

Cheesecake crown

For 6 you need

75 g (3 oz) vegetable margarine
175 g (6 oz) muesli cookies
1 × 142 g (5 oz) packet blackcurrant jelly, in pieces
1 × 150 g (5.29 oz) carton blackcurrant yoghurt
225 g (8 oz) low-fat soft cheese – use Quark, fromage blanc or curd cheese
1 egg white
12-14 rectangular ice cream wafers
1 × 240 g (8 oz) tube white icing
1 small packet Jelly tots

small saucepan ● plastic bag ● rolling pin ● wooden spoon ● measuring jug ● 15 cm (6 inch) deep, round loose-bottomed cake tin ● 2 mixing bowls ● metal spoon ● rotary or electric whisk ● round-bladed knife ● small kitchen knife

1 Turn on the oven to 200°C or 400°F or Gas Mark 6. Put the margarine into the saucepan and gently melt over a low heat.

2 Crush the cookies by putting them into the plastic bag and squashing them with the rolling pin. Add the biscuits to the melted margarine and mix well. Using the back of the wooden spoon press the mixture into the cake tin.

3 Put the jelly into the measuring jug and <u>carefully</u> add boiling water until you have 150 ml (¼ pint) of liquid. Boiling water can splash and give a nasty burn so it might be best to ask a grown-up to do this for you. Stir the jelly until it has dissolved and then stir in 150 ml (¼ pint) cold water. Let the jelly mixture get quite cool.

These look nice but ours taste better !

40

4 Put the yoghurt and cheese into the mixing bowl and stir well with a spoon. Whisk in the cooled jelly. Put the bowl in a cool place until the mixture starts to set.

5 Put the egg white into the second bowl and whisk it with a clean whisk until it is stiff. Fold it into the jelly mixture with the metal spoon. Pour the mixture into the cake tin and carefully put it in the refrigerator to set. (It will need about 6 hours but leave it there overnight if you can.)

6 Carefully run a round-bladed knife around the inside of the cake tin and then remove the cheesecake from the tin. Carefully cut the wafers to a point and arrange them around the cake to make a crown, pressing them on to the side and using a little of the white icing to stick them in place if necessary. Squeeze out small blobs of the icing and fix the Jelly tots in place on the wafers to look like jewels. It is best to eat this as soon as possible.

NOTE The best way to cut the wafers is to place them on a suitable cutting surface such as a wooden board. Then, with a kitchen knife, very carefully cut the wafers into a point as shown in the picture.

Below: A cheesecake crown surrounded by glittering jewels

Spaceman dips

Boost your next party into orbit with these delicious dips. Each dip serves 6-8 astronauts. They are all fun to make and even more fun to eat.

artian base

1 × 213 g (7½ oz) can pink salmon, drained and flaked
1 × 150 g (5.29 oz) carton natural yoghurt
1 tablespoon tomato purée
salt and pepper
1 tablespoon lemon juice
1 tablespoon wine vinegar
⅓ cucumber, diced
2 tablespoons freshly chopped parsley

mixing bowl ● wooden spoon ● cup

1 Put the salmon, yoghurt and tomato purée in the mixing bowl and stir with the wooden spoon to mix thoroughly.

2 Stir in salt and a dash of pepper to taste.

3 Mix the lemon juice and vinegar together in the cup and add enough to make the dip smooth but not too runny.

4 Just before serving stir in the cucumber and parsley. Serve the dip in a shallow bowl and supply bread sticks, carrot chunks and cucumber sticks for dipping.

5 Serve quickly or if making in advance stir every so often.

oon landing

2 large ripe bananas
1 × 240 g (8 oz) tub Greek-style yoghurt
1 teaspoon honey

TO DECORATE
1 banana (as straight as possible)
1 green glacé cherry (if liked)
2 fan wafers

mixing bowl ● fork ● wooden spoon ● wooden board ● small kitchen knife

1 Peel the bananas and put them in the mixing bowl. Using the fork, mash them well.

2 Stir in the yoghurt and honey and mix well with the wooden spoon. Spoon the dip into a serving bowl.

3 Decorate the dip. Peel the remaining banana and put it on a wooden board. <u>Carefully</u> cut a slice off one end so that it will stand, and trim it as straight as possible. Give it a green nose cone with the glacé cherry if you like.

4 Cut the fan wafers in half to make 4 fins and stand these around the banana as shown in the picture. Slices of apple, which have been dipped in lemon juice to stop them turning brown, make good, healthy dippers; so do sponge fingers.

Shuttle launch

6 eggs, hard-boiled
175 g (6 oz) low-fat soft cheese
4 tablespoons natural yoghurt
2-4 teaspoons tomato ketchup
salt and pepper

mixing bowl ● fork ● wooden spoon

1 Remove the shells from the hard-boiled eggs and put the eggs in the mixing bowl. Mash them thoroughly with the fork.

2 Stir in the soft cheese and yoghurt with the wooden spoon and mix very well.

3 Add enough of the tomato ketchup to turn the dip orange in colour and give it a good flavour. Add salt to taste and a dash of pepper if liked.

4 Serve the dip with breadsticks and vegetable dippers. Use cocktail sticks to spear pieces of vegetables.

From left: Martian base; Shuttle launch; Moon landing with a selection of dippers

Saucy sausages

akes 8

8 chipolata sausages
4 teaspoons sweet pickle
8 streaky bacon rashers, rinds cut off

wooden board • small serrated knife
• butter knife • rolling pin • wooden
cocktail sticks • baking sheet

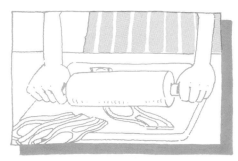

1 Put the sausages on the wooden board. Use the serrated (zig-zag) knife to <u>carefully</u> cut each sausage lengthways,

almost through to the bottom. Open out and spread the cut sides with a little pickle, then fold the sausages back together again.

2 Turn the oven on to 190°C or 375°F or Gas Mark 5. Put the bacon on the board and stretch and flatten each rasher by rolling it with the rolling pin. Wrap each filled sausage in a bacon rasher.

3 Push each sausage carefully on to a wooden cocktail stick. Put them on a baking sheet.

4 Bake the sausages for 20-25 minutes, turning the wooden cocktail sticks over carefully (<u>use oven mitts</u>) after 10 minutes. When they are cooked, carefully take the baking sheet out of the oven (<u>oven mitts again</u>) and use a fork to push the sausages off the wooden cocktail sticks on to a serving plate. Don't forget to turn the oven off.

Pancake letters

*A selection
of pancake letters*

M akes about 8

200 g (7 oz) self-raising flour
1 tablespoon sugar
1 egg, beaten
300 ml (½ pint) milk
oil for greasing

1 or 2 bowls ● balloon whisk ● sieve
● wooden spoon ● heavy frying pan
or griddle ● small jug ● round-bladed
knife

1 Put the flour and sugar into the bowl. Make a hole in the centre and pour in the egg and milk. With the balloon whisk beat the mixture well, until it looks smooth. If the mixture – called a batter – looks lumpy, just pour it through a sieve into another bowl, using the wooden spoon to help the mixture through. Now you need to get a grown-up to help you with all the rest, except the eating part!

2 Heat the heavy frying pan or griddle by putting it over medium heat for 2-3 minutes. Add about 1 teaspoon of oil and carefully tilt the pan a little to spread the oil all over the surface of the frying pan.

3 Using the small jug, scoop up some batter and pour on to the surface of the heavy frying pan in the shape of a letter. If they start to stick, add more oil. When bubbles appear on the surface, turn it over using the round-bladed knife. Cook the other side, until golden. Serve hot with jam or syrup.

Rainbow jelly

Plenty for 4

½ × 142 g (5 oz) packets lemon and
    raspberry jelly, in pieces
¾ × 142 g (5 oz) packet lime jelly, in
    pieces
1 banana
1 apple
2 oranges
100 g (4 oz) grapes

---

saucepan ● measuring jug ● 900 ml
(1½ pint) fluted mould ● serrated
kitchen knife ● bowl ● wooden
board ● teaspoon

3 Make the raspberry jelly in exactly the same way. When it is cool but not set, pour it gently on top of the lemon jelly in the mould. Put it back into the refrigerator until it has set.

1 Put the half packet of lemon jelly in a saucepan with 150 ml (¼ pint) water. Put the pan over a low heat, stirring now and then until all the jelly has dissolved. Carefully pour the jelly into the heatproof measuring jug and add cold water until you have 250 ml (8 fl oz) of liquid.

4 Repeat step 3, using lime jelly, but this time make the liquid up to 350 ml (12 fl oz). Pour it on top of the raspberry layer. Put it in the refrigerator until set.

2 Fill the fluted mould with cold water and then empty it. The little water that is left on the surface of the mould will help to stop the jelly sticking. Pour in the jelly mixture and put it in the refrigerator for about an hour until set.

THE JELLY'S SET!

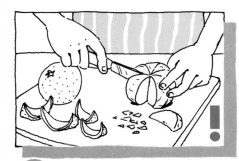

5 While the last jelly layer is setting, get the fruit ready. Peel and slice the banana and put it in the bowl. Core and carefully chop the apple (you don't need to peel it if you wash it well first). Then peel the oranges, remove the remaining white pith with the knife and carefully cut the oranges into segments. Do this on the wooden board. Add the apple and oranges to the banana with any juice from the oranges – this will help stop the bananas going brown. Carefully cut the grapes in half. Using the teaspoon, scoop out the seeds and add the grape halves to the bowl.

6 Fill the sink with hot water. Dip the mould in the hot water while you count to 5. Put a plate upside-down on top of the mould. Holding the mould and plate firmly together, turn them both over. The jelly should drop out on to the plate if you give the mould a gentle shake. If it doesn't, dip it in the hot water and try again. Serve the jelly with the fruit, either in a separate bowl or piled around or on top of the jelly.

PS Before you turn the jelly out of the mould it is a good idea to slightly wet the plate you plan to use. That way, if the jelly is not in the middle of the plate you can slide it into place.

When you serve the jelly to your friends or family it's great fun to buy all sorts of rainbow-coloured small presents like pencils, rubbers and hats for the party.

Below: A quivering Rainbow jelly surrounded by fresh fruit

Great day cakes

It's fun to make a special cake for a celebration but it is hard to keep it a secret if you have to spend a long time in the kitchen. The answer is to buy the basic cake but decorate it yourself. Here are two simple ideas that look spectacular. For fun, invent your own decoration ideas.

Flutterby cake

Covers 1 cake
1 small round raspberry jam sponge
   sandwich cake
25 g (1 oz) vegetable margarine
50 g (2 oz) icing sugar, sifted
1 teaspoon milk
about 12 small orange and lemon
   flavoured jelly slices
3 Matchmaker chocolate sticks, cut
   into approximately 5 cm (1 inch)
   lengths
1 candle holder with 1 candle

wooden board ● small bowl ●
wooden spoon ● round-bladed or
small palette knife ● fish slice

1 Unwrap the cake and put it on the wooden board.

Where are you going to hide the cake?

In my tummy

2 Make the icing by beating the margarine, icing sugar and milk together in a small bowl with a wooden spoon until smooth. Spread the icing over the top of the cake with the round-bladed or palette knife.

3 Make 6 butterfly patterns on the top of the cake using the orange and lemon slices and pieces of Matchmaker chocolate sticks (the picture shows you how).

4 Stick the candle holder and candle in the middle. Put the cake on a plate with the fish slice.

PS This makes a very good cake for Mother's Day or Father's Day. There are more ideas for making things for other people in the section on edible presents.

Right: Candle cake; Far right: Flutterby cake both deliciously decorated

Covers 1 cake

1 small round chocolate sponge
    sandwich cake
25 g (1 oz) vegetable margarine
50 g (2 oz) icing sugar, sifted
1 teaspoon milk
1 tablespoon drinking chocolate
3 orange or lemon flavoured jelly
    slices
3 Matchmaker chocolate sticks
3 red jelly diamonds
3 candles and candle holders

---

wooden board ● small bowl ●
wooden spoon ● round-bladed knife
● fish slice

1 Unwrap the cake and put it on the wooden board.

2 Make the icing as in step 2 for Flutterby cake. When it is smooth, stir in the drinking chocolate. Use the round-bladed knife to spread the icing over the top of the cake.

3 Carefully move the cake to a plate using the fish slice.

4 Make 3 candle patterns on the top of the cake (the picture shows you how). The candle bases are made from jelly slices, the candles are made from Matchmaker chocolate sticks (break them if they are too long) and the flames are red jelly diamonds.

5 Finish by arranging cake candles in holders above and below the made-up candles.

Creepy crawlies

These marzipan marvels are perfect for parties. Plant a snail on a dip or a spider on the sausage rolls and you may be sure of some interesting reactions. But the best news is that they are delicious to eat.

To make a snail, caterpillar, and spider you will need:

1 × 250 g (8 oz) packet golden or white marzipan
icing sugar, for dusting
brown, green and orange food colourings

TO DECORATE
Look at the recipes to see how to decorate each animal

You don't need any special utensils to make these – just a clean work surface dusted with icing sugar to stop the marzipan sticking. Use your hands to shape the marzipan. To divide the marzipan, cut the block in half and set one piece aside for the caterpillar. Cut the other half into 2, one piece for the spider and one piece for the snail. To colour the marzipan, add a few drops of your chosen food colouring to the marzipan. Press and mix the marzipan with your fingers until the colour is even. See step illustration on page 62.

Snail

1 small ball of marzipan (about the size of a walnut) for the body
1 ball of marzipan half the size of the body, for the shell
1 liquorice comfit, cut in half, for the eyes
liquorice bootlaces or sticks, for the feelers and mouth

1 Roll the body ball with your hands into a thick sausage, about 6 cm (2½ inches) long. Make a snout at one end and a point at the other end.

2 Colour the shell ball brown. Roll into a sausage 7.5 cm (3 inches) long. Roll into a coil, then press the shell gently on to the body.

3 Position the eyes on the thick end of the body. Cut 2 lengths of liquorice 1 cm (½ inch) and 1 of 5 mm (¼ inch) for the antennae and mouth. Stick on the body as shown in the picture.

aterpillar

6 walnut-sized marzipan balls for
   the body
12 liquorice comfits for the legs
2 pieces of marzipan, very thinly
   rolled, for the feelers
1 dolly mixture cut in half, for the eyes

1 Colour the body balls green
if you like. Roll them to even-
sized rounds and join them
together to make a curvy
caterpillar.

2 Use liquorice comfits to make
legs as shown in the picture.

3 Shape the marzipan feelers
and put them in position on
the head.

4 Finish the caterpillar by
adding the eyes.

pider

1 walnut-sized marzipan ball for
   the body
8 thin marzipan sausages, each
   about 4 cm (1½ inches) long, for
   the legs
1 orange liquorice comfit cut in half,
   for the eyes
1 small piece of marzipan, made into
   a sausage shape, for the mouth

1 Colour the marzipan body
orange and the marzipan
legs brown if you like.

2 Press one end of each spider
leg into the top of the body
and bend into shape to meet the
table, bending each leg up at the
end (the picture shows you how).
Press all the legs into position,
leaving a little gap at the front for
the eyes.

3 Place the liquorice comfit
eyes in place in the space
you have left. Try and make them
look like they are standing out on
stalks!

4 Shape the mouth and put it in
position.

Left: Creepy caterpillar; Middle: Spinny spider; Right: Slippery snail

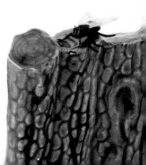

Mocktails

unk lady

For 6 you need
1 × 142 g (5 oz) packet lime flavoured
    jelly, in pieces
120 ml (4 fl oz) apple juice
120 ml (4 fl oz) concentrated
    blackcurrant drink
250 ml (8 fl oz) lemonade

TO DECORATE
6 red, 6 green and 6 yellow glacé
    cherries
wooden cocktail sticks

6 cocktail glasses ● 6 straws ● big
jug ● long-handled spoon

This makes a wonderful and very colourful drink for a party. Start making it the day before as the jelly needs time to set.

1 Make up the jelly according to the instructions on the packet. Let it cool a little and then pour it into 6 cocktail glasses. Each glass should be just under half full. Put the glasses in the refrigerator. Add a straw to each glass, at an angle. The straws tend to pop out but will stay in position if you prop them against a bottle or tall jar. Let the jelly set for at least 6 hours or overnight. As it sets the straws will become firmly anchored.

2 Just before you plan to serve the punk ladies, make the decoration. Stick 1 red, 1 green and

1 yellow glacé cherry on to a cocktail stick. You can, if you like, make them look like traffic lights – don't forget to get the order right.

3 In the big jug mix the apple juice and concentrated blackcurrant drink. Pour in the lemonade.

4 Carefully pour the bright red juice into each glass. Then place your cherry decoration across the top of each glass. You can't drink through the straw of course, but it looks great! When you've finished the juice use a spoon to scoop up the jelly.

℗op pinacolada

Enough for 4
2 × 150 g (5.29 oz) cartons coconut
    and pineapple yoghurt
2 yoghurt cartons pineapple juice
4 yoghurt cartons lemonade

large jug ● rotary or electric whisk

This drink is very easy to make as you use one of the empty yoghurt cartons as a measure — it saves time on washing up, too!

1 Put all the ingredients in the jug and whisk until the mixture is all bubbly and frothy. Pour into 4 glasses and serve straight away.

ocha malted milkshakes

Makes 4
1 litre (1¾ pints) cold skimmed milk
8 tablespoons chocolate syrup
4 teaspoons instant coffee powder
4 teaspoons sugar
4 tablespoons malted milk powder

large jug ● rotary or electric whisk

1 Put all the ingredients in the jug and whisk until frothy. Pour into 4 tall glasses and serve straight away.

For a change you can sprinkle the surface of each drink with a little grated chocolate, or a scoop of ice-cream for an extra treat.

Frothy cocktails from left: Mocha malted milkshake; Pop pinacolada; Punk lady

Gift wrapping

Edible gifts go down well, in every way. Homemade sweets, biscuits and cakes are always popular and they show you care enough to spend time as well as money on the presents you choose to give. You can wrap them beautifully, too — and without spending a lot of money. The gingerbread robot looks good on a silver board, but there's no need to go to the expense of buying one. Cut out a piece of firm cardboard (the side panel from a large box will do if it is clean). The piece of card should be larger than the robot and you can make it any shape you like — a larger version of the robot would look terrific. Wrap it in foil, sticking it down with tape on the side you won't see. Put the robot

on the board and then cover it with cling film (also taped underneath). For a birthday gift you could cover the board in appropriate wrapping paper.

You can make presentation boxes from yoghurt pots, ice cream boxes (plastic ones) or margarine tubs covered in foil, crêpe paper, or cellophane. Newspaper is a bit messy but brightly coloured magazine pages are very useful — a cone made from a children's magazine makes a good container for biscuits, hard sweets or cheese twists.

The decorated eggs look great in a painted egg box, and you could present chocolate truffles in a mug to make a double present.

Dominoes

This makes about 20

200 g (7 oz) self-raising flour
25 g (1 oz) cornflour
100 g (4 oz) butter or solid margarine
100 g (4 oz) caster sugar
1 small egg, beaten
a few drops of vanilla essence
1 × 100 g (4 oz) packet plain
    chocolate drops

large bowl ● wooden spoon ● rolling
pin ● fish slice ● greased baking
sheet ● small knife

1 Mix the flour and cornflour in the bowl. Rub in the butter and stir in the sugar, egg and vanilla essence with a wooden spoon. Knead gently until you have a smooth dough.

2 Sprinkle a clean work surface and the rolling pin with a little flour. Roll out the dough to a rectangle about 5 mm (¼ inch)

thick. Cut into bars of about 3.5 cm × 7 cm (1½ × 3 inches). Use the fish slice to lift the bars on to the greased baking sheet. Leave a little space between the bars.

3 Turn on the oven to 180°C or 350°F or Gas Mark 4. Mark each bar in half with the back of the knife. Arrange chocolate drops on each half to look like domino dots.

4 Put the baking sheet in the oven and bake the dominoes for about 15 minutes. Carefully take them out of the oven (use oven mitts) and leave them to cool slightly on the sheet before using the fish slice to move them to a wire rack to cool completely. Turn the oven off. Wrap the biscuits.

Gingerbread robot

akes 1

100 g (4 oz) plain flour
½ teaspoon bicarbonate of soda
½ teaspoon ground ginger
½ teaspoon ground cinnamon
25 g (1 oz) vegetable margarine
50 g (2 oz) soft brown sugar
2 tablespoons golden syrup
1 teaspoon milk

TO DECORATE:
a little icing sugar
white marzipan
apricot jam
liquorice shoelaces
silver balls
wine gum shapes
liquorice comfits
240 g (8 oz) tube royal icing
dolly mixtures
liquorice allsorts
crystallized orange slice

28 × 18 cm (11 × 7 inch) greased
baking sheet ● pencil ● tracing
paper ● thin cardboard ● scissors ●
sieve ● large bowl ● saucepan ●
wooden spoon ● plastic bag ● rolling
pin ● small sharp knife ● pastry
brush ● wire rack

1 Prepare the robot cut-out by following instructions on page 58.

2 Sift the flour, soda and spices into the large bowl. Put the margarine, sugar and syrup into the saucepan and place over a low heat until melted. Take the pan off

the heat (use oven mitts) and then you *must* let the mixture cool. Make a hole in the middle of the flour mixture and pour in the cool syrup mixture. Beat well with the wooden spoon until it forms a firm dough. With your hands, knead the mixture very lightly until it is smooth. Put the dough in the plastic bag and place in the refrigerator for 30 minutes until it's quite cool.

3 Turn on the oven to 160°C or 325°F or Gas Mark 3. Sprinkle a little flour on your work surface and rolling pin. Roll out the dough until it is as thin as a 10p piece. Lightly flour the robot cut-out and place it on the dough. Carefully cut round it, using the small knife. Slide the robot shape on to the greased baking sheet and brush with milk using the pastry brush. Put it in the oven to bake for 10-15 minutes or until the robot is firm. Using oven mitts, remove the sheet from the oven and carefully slide the robot on to the wire rack to cool. Turn off the oven. The robot spreads during cooking by about 1 cm (½ inch) all round.

4 Sprinkle a little icing sugar on your working surface and (clean) rolling pin. Roll out the marzipan to the same thickness as the dough. Place the cut-outs for the panels on to the marzipan, making sure they have been dusted with icing sugar first, and, using the small knife, <u>carefully</u> cut round them. Stick in position, as in the picture, with a thin coating of apricot jam.

5 Cut the shoelaces into 3 × 1 cm (½ inch) lengths and push them into the head panel with silver balls between them. Stick wine gums, comfits and silver balls into the control panel and knee pads using the tube of icing.

6 To make the eyes use dolly mixtures with a white centre. The nose is a liquorice allsort and the mouth is an orange jelly slice. The epaulettes are quartered liquorice allsorts.

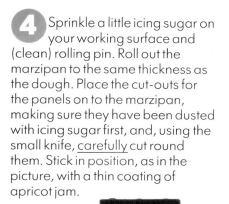

Above left: Gift-wrapped Ginger-bread robot; Above: Cooked Ginger-bread robot

GINGERBREAD ROBOT CUT-OUT

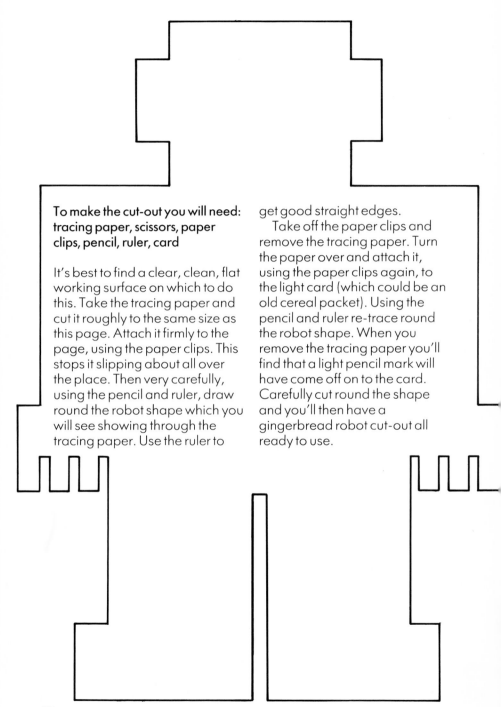

To make the cut-out you will need: tracing paper, scissors, paper clips, pencil, ruler, card

It's best to find a clear, clean, flat working surface on which to do this. Take the tracing paper and cut it roughly to the same size as this page. Attach it firmly to the page, using the paper clips. This stops it slipping about all over the place. Then very carefully, using the pencil and ruler, draw round the robot shape which you will see showing through the tracing paper. Use the ruler to get good straight edges.

Take off the paper clips and remove the tracing paper. Turn the paper over and attach it, using the paper clips again, to the light card (which could be an old cereal packet). Using the pencil and ruler re-trace round the robot shape. When you remove the tracing paper you'll find that a light pencil mark will have come off on to the card. Carefully cut round the shape and you'll then have a gingerbread robot cut-out all ready to use.

Stripy cheese twists

Makes about 24

100 g (4 oz) plain flour plus a little for
    sprinkling
pinch of mustard
50 g (2 oz) butter or solid margarine
50 g (2 oz) Cheddar, Edam or Gouda
    cheese
4 teaspoons cold water
1-2 tablespoons Marmite

large bowl ● grater ● wooden spoon
● rolling pin ● butter knife ● 2 baking
sheets

1 Sift the flour and mustard into the bowl. Rub in the butter or margarine. Finely grate the cheese. Stir it into the flour mixture with the wooden spoon.

2 Stir in the water and then shape the mixture to a ball. Sprinkle your working surface and rolling pin with flour and roll out the dough to a rectangle, about 25 × 15 cm (10 × 6 inches). Using the butter knife, spread the dough with the Marmite. Turn the oven on to 190°C or 375°F or Gas Mark 5.

3 Fold the dough over once so that the Marmite is inside. Roll out the dough to a rectangle again and cut it into 12 strips. Cut the strips in half horizontally and carefully shape each strip into a twist. Arrange the cheese twists on the baking sheets.

4 Put the baking sheets in the oven and bake the twists for 10-12 minutes until they are golden. Carefully take the sheets out of the oven (use oven mitts). Turn the oven off. Let the twists cool before packing them.

Below: Stripy cheese twists

Choc-orange truffles

Makes about 450 g (1 lb)

100 g (4 oz) plain chocolate, broken
100 g (4 oz) soft unsalted butter
275 g (10 oz) icing sugar
1 teaspoon orange juice
1 teaspoon grated orange rind
chocolate sugar strands or cocoa
    powder to cover

---

saucepan ● metal spoon ● large
bowl ● wooden spoon ● teaspoon ●
soup plate ● paper sweet cases

1 Put the chocolate into the saucepan over a low heat until it's melted, stirring with the metal spoon.

2 Beat the butter in the bowl with the wooden spoon. Stir in the melted chocolate and the icing sugar, mixing well. Beat in the orange juice and rind. Put the bowl in the refrigerator for 45 minutes until the mixture is stiff.

3 Take the bowl out of the refrigerator and, using the teaspoon, scoop out small amounts of the mixture and roll them into balls.

4 Cover the bottom of the soup plate with chocolate sugar strands or cocoa powder. Add the balls, a few at a time and shake the plate until the balls are coated in chocolate or cocoa. Pop each chocolate orange truffle into a paper sweet case and arrange them in a box or on a tray. Keep in the refrigerator until needed.

Decorated eggs

For 3 eggs

3 brown eggs, hard-boiled
240 g (8 oz) tube royal icing

AN ASSORTMENT OF THE
  FOLLOWING
black liquorice sticks
liquorice shoelaces
liquorice comfits
liquorice allsorts

FOR THE CAT
1 jelly diamond

FOR THE CLOWN
coloured shredded paper
2 dolly mixtures
1 Smartie
1 lemon jelly slice

FOR THE GRANNY
1 white marshmallow
few coconut strands
2 silver balls

Above: Three decorated eggs
Left: A box of Choc-orange truffles

1 For the features look at the picture and use the tube of icing to stick on the appropriate sweets and use coloured felt pens for extra detail on the faces.

2 For the whiskers on the cat, cut the liquorice shoelace into 6 × 2 cm (¾ inch) pieces. Stick 3 on each side of the egg, with the icing. Stick a liquorice allsort and the jelly diamond in position in the same way.

3 For the clown's hair, put a blob of icing on top of the egg then neatly gather a few strands of paper in your hand. Find the centre of the paper then stick it down on to the icing. Add an allsort for the hat.

4 For granny's glasses make two loopy knots in a liquorice shoelace. Place them on the egg (see picture) and then tie in a knot at the back to secure the glasses firmly in place.

Hearts and flowers

Peppermint flowers

Makes about 20
1 egg white
450 g (1 lb) icing sugar
few drops of peppermint essence
few drops of green food colouring
1 small packet silver balls

2 large bowls ● rotary whisk ● sieve
● teaspoon ● rolling pin ● flower-
shaped cutters ● baking sheet

1 In a large bowl lightly whisk the egg white until it becomes slightly frothy.

2 In the other bowl sift the icing sugar through the sieve. Then gradually add enough egg white and peppermint essence to make a cushiony paste.

3 Sprinkle your work surface with icing sugar and put the fondant mixture on it. Knead it for a few minutes, then add a few drops of green colouring by placing a few drops in the teaspoon, then adding the colouring from the teaspoon to the fondant mixture a drop at a time. Carry on kneading until all the fondant mixture is coloured green. Using the rolling pin coated in icing sugar, gently roll it out until it is 5 mm (¼ inch) thick. Cut out flower shapes (if you keep dipping the cutters in icing sugar it will be easier to remove the flowers).

4 Put the sweets on the baking sheet and stick a silver ball on each of the petals. Let the flowers dry out for 2-3 days before packing them into boxes or decorated cartons to give as gifts.

This doesn't let them off the washing up.

# **O**range hearts

Makes about 15
25 g (1 oz) low-fat soft cheese
finely grated rind of 1 orange
275 g (10 oz) icing sugar
few drops of orange food colouring

bowl ● wooden spoon ● sieve ●
rolling pin ● heart-shaped cutters ●
baking sheet

1 In the bowl beat the soft
cheese and finely grated
orange rind with the wooden
spoon until the mixture is soft. Sift
the icing sugar into the same bowl
and beat into the cheese until you
get a soft, manageable mixture.

2 Sprinkle your work surface
with icing sugar and put the
fondant mixture on it. Knead it

gently and then add a few drops of
the orange food colouring (see
step illustration). Carry on
kneading the mixture until it is pale
orange in colour.

3 Using the rolling pin dusted in
icing sugar, gently roll it out
until it is 5 mm (¼ inch) thick. Cut out
the heart shapes using the cutters
that have been dipped in icing
sugar. Set the sweets aside on the
baking sheet to dry for 2-3 days.

*Below: Prettily packed Peppermint
flowers and Orange hearts*

Index

Apple:
  Indian apples 31

Baked potatoes and fillings 24-6
Banana:
  Bikers bananas 28
  Loch Ness monster 38
  Moon landing dip 42
Beating 8
Beef:
  Jungleburgers 20-1
Biscuits:
  Dominoes 55
  Stripy cheese twists 59
BMX baps 29
Buttons and bows 18

Cakes:
  Candle cake 49
  Flutterby cake 48
  Fudge brownies 30
Caterpillar (marzipan) 51
Cheese:
  BMX baps 29
  Stripy cheese twists 59
  Totem rolls 33
Cheesecake crown 40-1
Chicken:
  Chicken in a ring 27
  Chunky chicken soup 13
  Tom-tom (chicken)
    drumsticks 32
Choc-orange truffles 60
Cooking terms 8-11
Coring 8
Cowboy pies 22
Cyclops specials 19

Dicing 9
Dips 42-3
Dominoes (biscuits) 55
Draining 9
Drinks for parties 52-3
Drizzling 9

Egg:
  To break an egg 10
  Cyclops specials 19
  Decorated eggs 61
  Egg and tuna triple-deckers
    28

Shuttle launch dip 43

Flaking 9
Flutterby cake 48
Folding 9
Fruity fools 37
Fudge brownies 30

Gift wrappings for edible gifts 54
Gingerbread robot 56-8
Grating 9
Greasing 10

Hearts and flowers (sweets) 62-3
Hunky hot hats 23

Igloo puddings 36
Indian apples 31

Jungleburgers 20-1

Kitchen code 6-7
Kneading 10

Loch Ness monster 38

Marble fondue 39
Martian base dip 42
Marzipan creepy crawlies 50-1
Measuring 8
Mocha malted milkshakes 53
Mocktails 52-3
Moon landing dip 42

Orange hearts (sweets) 63

Pancake letters 45
Pasta:
  Buttons and bows 18
  Seaside salad 12
Peppermint flowers (sweets) 62
Picnic food 28-33
Pittas 16-17
Pop pinacolada 52
Popeye power pack pittas 16
Potato:
  Baked potatoes and fillings
    24-6
Puddings:
  Cheesecake crown 40-1

Fruity fools 37
Igloo puddings 36
Indian apples 31
Loch Ness monster 38
Marble fondue 39
Rainbow jelly 46-7
Sci-fi trifle 34-5
Punk lady (drink) 52

Quiche-me-quicks 14-15

Rainbow jelly 46-7
Rolling 10
Rubbing in 11

Saddlebag specials 28-30
Safety reminders 6
Salmon:
  Buttons and bows 18
  Martian base dip 42
Sausage, sausagemeat:
  Cowboy pies 22
  Saucy sausages 44
  Sausage surprise pittas 16
Sci-fi trifle 34-5
Seaside salad 12
Separating 11
Shuttle launch dip 43
Sifting 11
Simmering 11
Snail (marzipan) 50
Soup:
  Chunky chicken soup 13
Spider (marzipan) 51
Sweets:
  Choc-orange truffles 60
  Orange hearts 63
  Peppermint flowers 62

Tom-tom drumsticks 32
Totem rolls 33
Trifle 34-5
Truffles 60
Tuna:
  Buttons and bows 18
  Egg and tuna triple-deckers
    28
  Seaside salad 12

Whisking 11
Wigwam wonders 31-3